You Are Indeed an Elk, But This is Not The Forest You Were Born to Graze

Kyle McCord

ISBN 13: 978-0-692-30941-4

ISBN 10: 0692309411

Cover design by Brian Mihok

Cover art: "The Ship of Fools" Robyn O'Neil

Gold Wake Press Collective

Boston, MA

You Are Indeed an Elk, But This is Not The Forest You Were Born to Graze

Poems

One

Two

I. This is Not the Forest

[I had no intention to retire from soothsaying]

I had no intention
to retire from soothsaying,
and that was the first
of my numerous problems.
Also, I'd been a stowaway
scrounging vermin
on the swanboat of the dead
since the church first forbade
hippopotamus interruptus.
One day, I'd be instructed
to recycle glass products
in the blue or gray bins,
and the next some scoundrel
would be all up in my weave.
Then the cannons socking endlessly
into the late afternoon
while we rounded the cape,
the tea leaves scoffing
at the labradoodle which flew
its tongue like a flag.
Likely I hadn't the slightest clue
that what open-throttled toward me

wasn't hankering to save me.
But why would I?
The same thing that broke
a foyer window in mid-autumn
made a superb gift
for my friend, the mason.
Inside me was one insatiable radiance
after another.

[Put down that pint of human blood and tell me you need me]

Put down that pint of human blood
and tell me you need me.
You've no idea where that's been,
and this hell is a hell of sawdust
and grumpy bassoons.
Today we're dozing
beside the hoarders like obese antelope,
tomorrow I'm shaking the maraca of darkness
for your lost innocence like you like.
When your jasmine blossom
wafts through the valleys,
I am a landscape
undergoing the most intimate
types of erosion.
You say, Let's slow down,
find a motel
with dewy grasses enough
to slavishly lick these sores.
But such ecstatic sensations are dangerous
even for residents of Defiance, Ohio.
Our chains could cause dolphin injuries.
Your wings could crush girders.

The guidebook says
this hell is a hell of lovers
genuflecting
in their flashy wristwatches.
What else did you hope it would say?
Put away your ethereal stemware,
come whisper with me
beside the river of idle lies?
Set aside your ragged books, you beg,
return to bed beside the water.
Here, we become the alternate endings
of our own low-budget dreams.
We look around at the ash
snowing into the tree line.
The wind catches remnants
of a terrarium in its blaze
whirring each into heartbreak
just as you wish.

[Last night I heard the frail music of nighthawks]

Last night I heard the frail
music of nighthawks.
Like an amateur imperialist,
my life envelopes the outdoors.
One nighthawk I name
Judas Squawking Priest
to honor the wishes
of your deceased rabbit hutch.
Had its injuries been less severe,
less self-inflicted,
we might be daydreaming
of housing loans together.
We might have finally made it
were it not for that thunder over there
cowing all the animal actors.
But why even bother now?
I've confided so much to you
though you're just a toothpick
slash makeshift lawn dart
slash festive dwarf umbrella.
You remind me of my years
as a stunt double

for abandoned apartments.
On the side, I was a stand-in
for the arm hair
of a thousand-year-old shepherdess.
I'd tow cars after hours
to the Scared Straight program.
While they might have
resented it at the time,
I wouldn't be the hawk I am today
without my masters.
One gaze and the world
crawls back into its cannon
like an acrobat
enshrining herself
in the lion's mouth.

[This is no time for grandiose displays of pinball prowess]

This is no time for grandiose
displays of pinball prowess.
Those mutants will be hitching up
the driveway any minute
and I intend to be ready
with some meat tongs
and a jug of kerosene nightmares
like the born-again survivalist I am.
This is no time for multi-ball
here in the basement
even if you've nearly
unlocked makeout point.
Upstairs are the man-eaters
and their pal Susie
the sewer alligator
licking the last of her incisors
she hasn't already swallowed,
baby birds shrieking up daylight.
Where's the bravery I saw
in this ghostwritten memoir
of your life as a movie gaffer?
On page forty-three, you write

When I'd seen enough
coffee fetchers tased
I knew I needed out
of this unaired Brady Bunch episode
to which I was slave.
I still have a thorn inside me
from my days as the keygrip's bard.
I won't apologize for it.
I'm not going out
like some swanky lounge lamp
while those mutants have their way
with the off-brand furniture
to the sounds of early Lou Reed.
It's time to dust off
that whirring propeller
you call the human spirit.
There's getting to know your body
then there's living in it.
I breezed into this world
with a wolf in my suede jacket
and I intend to go out the same way:
sorry, gored, with meat tongs
dripping down my fingers,
and only a love
of digitally inserted heartache
to keep me.

[When a man loves a woman, he sits her down]

When a man loves a woman,
he sits her down and grasps her hand
in the manner one might hold a seashell.
Darling, he says, I confess
I've felt my whole life
like a serpent among babies
in a barren waste of human excrement.
To which the beloved shall nod.
To which the studio audience
shall be instructed to brutishly shout.
To which a mighty army of the dead
shall be conjured to Skull Mountain.
And distantly a black wave
clacks its tongue against a sea cave.
No, no, the painter thinks
and reaches into his wicker basket.
He paints a crib at the crest of the wave,
a crib at the trough.
A throng of babies
will overtake this beach, he thinks,
but at least I'll die beautiful.
The woman reenters the portrait

to find her lover lost in thought.
Darling, says the woman,
bending to her knees,
I confess for as long as I've known you,
I've been a pine
chopped down
and loaded onto a truck
for a Christmas extravaganza.
When I breathe, I can feel tinsel
flooding my lungs.
When you prune me,
I can make out the voices of carolers
fleeing the fjord.
And they fall into each other
like clumsy ghosts—
the man shimmying his rattle,
the woman dropping her cones.

[If you won't swear to remarry me in the afterlife]

If you won't swear
to remarry me in the afterlife,
we will both surely die
in this cornfield.
The thresher is abuzz
with alien searchlights.
Expand your view
of the marital compact,
or prepare to die,
comes the crackling voice
of the alien overlord
over an '80s boombox.
From your impudent stare,
your drawn Saturday Night Special,
I'm guessing the easy way out
is not so easy.
One thing I've learned
about being an intern
cold calling the Detroit metroplex
is you're always at a party
stepping on someone else's Maglite.
Or you're trapped in a cornfield,

hiding beneath a bailer.
Your appropriately-timed
Talmud references
won't save you,
cries the overlord.
His skiff of giant cats whirs.
I can practically hear your hate
somersaulting through your blood.
We will both surely die, I know.
Then, at that moment,
a shooting star
lights up the firs,
vowing me
the worst possible wish.

[Once they evacuate the impromptu rodeo]

Once they evacuate
the impromptu rodeo
there'll just be you, me,
and this can of white albacore.
We'll loot the t-shirt vendors
and divvy up private holdings
among the bovine class.
Our days boiling
Def Leppard eight-tracks
for sustenance
and stripping chandeliers
can finally end.
No more listless nights
with one eye on the tar pits,
another on the Anubian cultists
whose obsession with papier-mâché
long ago crested into the eerie.
No more waking to find the lawn
covered in jackal statues.
We'll gaze on the receding lights
of the stockyard
with the wild abandon
once reserved for dogs
trapped in tennis ball factories.

Did I mention the games?
No more saucy children
sassing the skee ball machines.
Just the good life
immolating all the gazebos
and felling whichever idols
we love the most.

[Even when I solicited Satan with affordable snow tires, he listened]

Even when I solicited Satan
with affordable snow tires,
he listened.
He looked on
while I buried my pet
anaphora Scampers
with a trowel and vengeful spirit.
He excused my general motif
of intercellular decay.
But when I lie to Satan,
he travels to Tibet to find himself.
He's like a sad sitar
turned to a life of busking.
When he levitates
back through the foyer
he has smugged up,
offers wisdom like:
The cup you attempt to fill
has no bottom.
At what are you aiming
with these mammalian
acrobatic performances?

He will never know
what is right again.
Maybe you, you out there,
have lost someone also.
Maybe you met your friends
while serving
as an overzealous display cake.
You don't deserve the name
Sarah "Rink Master" Bower
when you've allowed Zambonis
to menace your friends.
But this solar predator
which fords eons of asteroids
bumping and grinding
to die with you, forgives you.
You are king
of the amateur hockey circuit.
You have so much to live for.

[On my bucket list: don't do anything miraculous]

On my bucket list:
don't do anything miraculous
until at least some
of the wolf-children
cluster around my cage.
Until the enclosure light blinks green,
no pennies pulled from albatross eggs,
no transubstantiation
of cigarillos to armadillos
no matter who's on the bill.
I recognized long ago
that this is what would ruin me:
my adoration of the invisible.
On my bucket list:
host an incorporeal award show.
The award for most inept marketing
goes to the yeti
for his continued nonexistence
in the face of synergistic tie-ins.
Who knows—
maybe he's better off
in the 2 a.m. beer hall

of the human imagination.
Amidst the telescoping heat,
wolf-children circumnavigate my cage
like listless predator drones.
I find a darkness to carry
then I carry it.
The genius of my captivity
may not be clear to you now.
But like my annual
dark matter birthday blowout,
at least there'll be cake left over.
And I'll save one piece for the interns
closest to starvation
and another for you
and miscount a rosary
for all this avian splendor
flying in unfettered
nova form above.

[Perhaps this day marks the end of your kayak internship]

Perhaps this day marks the end
of your kayak internship,
but we'll always have
the unspeakable acts of kindness
we committed together.
All those hours spent
thrashing beneath the bulrushes,
overburdened with brochures
for Darrell's Ferret Park.
You've become like the felonious
philosophy tutor I never had.
You shed your life jacket
the way others shed
burning headdresses.
In shadowy bars
in the Berkshires,
the campers whimper
in hushed tones.
How many days
I've lived a catalog of scarcities
while exhaustion died out of you!
I'd like to apologize

for the merciless waterboarding
which followed.
As part of this internship,
I must demand you not
disclose your birth
and subsequent life.
Your days knotting dull winters
into hair are over.
Beyond them: further kayaks
of dubious legal origin,
a sandbar, a shoreline
rising like a wolf
to meet you.

II. You Are
Indeed an Elk

[I'd like to take a moment to honor the ordinary]

I'd like to take a moment to honor
the ordinary commotion
of these rhododendrons,
the snarky horn of the rhombus,
the corporation like a man in a bear suit
passed out in a mall.
I would like to take a moment
to inter-dimensionally chide
those time travelers
blaring their outer-city hip-hop
into the nation's protected marshlands.
The millionaire's speech
on austerity at the steel mill
like a sales pitch to top predators
on a book of love languages
ignored all warning signs:
the fierce snarls,
the worried glances from Wikipedia.
Vertical lakes drummed
inside your iris.
I'd like to take a moment
to honor the following love languages:

gift giving,
horse thievin',
affectionate deck swabbing.
Anyone joining us
from the underworld
is now invited
to sext the beloved.
Then this tour will continue
to the gift shop
before bursting
like an intestine of the sun.

[In this scene, my co-pilot and I crash the moonbuggy]

In this scene, my co-pilot
and I crash the moonbuggy
into the Cretaceous Period.
Listen to the way I soften my O's
when I scream into the headset,
Houston, we have a prehistoric problem!
That sort of enthusiasm is what separates
Copenhagen community theater
from the late Danish masters.
In these lectures, I've expounded
on that dappled marble we call memory.
I've disabled the regret machine
defectively spewing from my chest.
Like a weak-willed forest fire,
I've spread only that ruin
which I believed beneficial.
Once, as a student,
I fell into a deep sleep
during a public showing
of Triumph of the Will.
Asleep through the deafening marches,
iron eagles crowding the lens,

asleep through the next two decades
until a loose chandelier collapsed
rousing me.
Around me, the sleeping bodies
of my fellow moviegoers
heaped the carpet.
In this scene from Dino Disaster 5,
I tap into those stolen years.
Watch my lip quiver
as I unhitch my raptor bike
for one more ride.
As I deliver the titular line
This ain't no time-spill,
it's a dino disaster,
the tears you see are real,
the ghosts moonlighting
in the camera's cavernous afterglow.

[When a man loves a woman, they journey]

When a man loves a woman, they journey
into the Cleveland, Ohio of their youths.
What better way to greet these weary pilgrims
than Key Tower, the Western Reserve,
exceptional K-12 education?
Deeply discounted motels
raise their savage maws in approval.
Here, in a darkened room,
the lovers perform a dance
called the Hungry Tiger.
Even an unsilenced cellphone,
a bully loudly slicing
a sandwich with scissors,
could ruin this crystalline ritual.
You may be the finest Inuit boot model
ever to two-step it across the tundra,
but even the strongest succumb.
Sound the bellwether alarm
if you like,
but if you're meant to tiger,
you'll tiger.
These lovers must log eons
of rehearsal and recording hours
before they ascend the mountain

of public betrayal.
There, the man and woman
enter the holy computer lab
to post pictures of the dance.
Like a photon which feels fat
as both a particle and wave,
they regret and accept their betrayal
the instant of its occurrence.
But regret is only another step
in the Hungry Tiger.
Like pocketing pens
at an orthodontist's office,
carpet-bombing a horticultural exam,
making air quotes at a man
with his sleeve stuck in a bin
of binder clips,
or watching beauty
fade out of the world
while the storm turns west
over the Baltic.

[If you're reading this, I forgive you for eating me first]

If you're reading this,
I forgive you for eating me first.
Then Hector, our Mayan tour guide,
who doubtlessly ascended
the tree of wisdom
next to the fern of unwise disrobing
in public venues.
Then at least four members
of the archeology club
while those scrappy kids
obediently translated
the sarcophagus's inscription:
Please visit the gift shop
on your way out, vile desecrators.
I toot my rustic horn in approval.
If you're reading this,
beware Bachelor #1
whose love of long walks on sandy beaches
doesn't survive the second date.
Then the children come out of cryo
like greyhounds bounding
onto an orbital platform.

Bachelor #2,
the fleshless beast of nightmares,
shares your affection
for early Will Smith cinema
and couch surfing at polar research stations.
When the wind rushes over his billboard
empire, he secretes a sort of melancholy.
Rest assured, the SWAT teams
have him surrounded.
As for my effects,
buried beneath
our makeshift mackerel factory,
you'll find an alarmingly detailed biography
of Boris Kasparov
and a pictorial history of our years
as star-gazing antlers.
Scatter my leftovers
on the snow-drifted sea
where we birthed our young
and each day raised them
to be the most well-mannered people-eaters
ever to grace the stage.

[It was in those days]

It was in those days
that our general concocted his plan
to catapult corpses into the parapet
until the enemy surrendered.
The recalcitrant spirit
of some Massachusetts governor
popped through the porthole
of the general's dreams,
licking its ethereal thumbs,
slicking back its rattail.
After that,
we were really measuring and sawing
like belligerent little latitudes.
The thing about launching
decaying bodies
into a besieged city
is your soul
finds ways to mend,
said the general, off-hand.
As if those weren't the words
we had kept our fathers
ambulatory to hear.
Later we compared
various versions of the event

like bystanders scoring a shoot-out.
We found traitors to trebuchet
and we trebucheted them.
The general returned
to loudly sipping some broth.
Then the rain really broke loose
like the swift brushstrokes
of Japanese landscapes.

[I swear this is the last time I'm going into space]

I swear this is the last time
I'm going into space.
Whenever some warlike pack of cannibals
comes sailing through the cosmos,
I come to tangled in a parachute
nettled by prickly flora.
Is this the planet with the leopards
intent on undermining human liberty
or the one with the death ray
blithely swinging into position?
This is the type of question I often engage.
I feel like a guerrilla army
gassing up at the Stop N' Save.
How I will miss the way
you'd solder solar panels
with your amazing, little hands,
streak grease expertly across your uniform.
This is the last time I dream
of a life selling erections
to the elderly.
In this particular sector,
maybe no one's buying

the chemical brouhaha I'm pushing,
but I know I was born
for more than utility.
Night pushes its cool fingers
behind my ears.
Whenever I see some cowhand
with his boot on the tail
of an interstellar feline,
I'll stare up into the cosmological labyrinth.
Whenever I see the shivs
of alien fortifications
looming in my crosshairs,
I will think only of you.

[The snow whirs like another planet's machinery]

The snow whirs like another planet's
machinery gearing up one hootenanny
of a storm front.
If we must stay the night in this cabin
commemorating the short, brutish life
of Luke "Land Mine Tester" Tanner,
let's at least shut
the malevolent puppet display case.
I don't like the look of Big Wattle there,
flashing his giblets and brandishing
the Thigh Master with an air of menace.
I'm not fond of the alien replicants
nursing a grudge over the defenestration
and decapitation incident,
which I hope we can all concede
was an unfavorable way
for the birthday celebration to begin.
As an alien replicant yourself
inhabiting the body of a husky,
what safety issues seem most relevant?
Times like these, it feels strange
to call myself a lobbyist

for the Coalition for Clandestine Dentistry.
Sometimes I want to just cash it all in
and drill cavities in an occluded cave.
While we're on the topic of caving,
could we perhaps plug the crevice
with the pixies
foisting the power sander?
Yes, I can see you over there,
digging for a three-pronged adapter.
And I must admit,
I admire the tenacity
with which you beguile intruders
and also the spirit of teamwork
which has become the touchstone
of your current business-model.

[You can redeem yourself by helping me slay]

You can redeem yourself
by helping me slay
the population of Michigan
or just sit there like some military outpost
with its best days behind it, you said.
But with my mouth overflowing
with cubes of Gruyere
it was tough to tell you anything.
In the yard,
the dead drifted toward the house
jangling their martini ice
and generally making a mess
of the volleyball court.
There was this campfire smell
permeating our every thought,
which piled guests' plates
into funeral pyres.
Everything up to this point
had been part of our destiny:
to serve as hired dinner guests
while we regained our strength.
But the harpist gently strumming

inside your capillaries
had changed her tune.
Soon, I knew,
I would need to turn
my magic against you.
I looked into my palms
inventorying all I'd lost:
some henchmen,
a block of Gruyere,
an anxiety over the way
light watches over us.
A great disappointment
snaked about the carpet,
stripping decorum out of all conversations.
But decorum may be all I have
and all that will claim me,
and not even you
can take it from me, ghouls.

[Last night I heard the yowls of the listless jaguar]

Last night I heard the yowls
of the listless jaguar.
It was like goodbye itself
expertly sighing
Adios, amores.
For five years,
I served as an artistic rendering
of a radar station.
The lagoon accompanied
my pantomime,
crashing images of clouds.
I remember another sundown
when you and I were cousins.
The moon, that luminous bear rug
looming down on our bodies.
Promise never to forget
how eagerly we paraded
among those ziggurats,
flutter-tonguing our trumpets
as though we owned the place,
as though we were not sorry

for all the noble terror
swelling inside us.

[For the sake of this mathematical hypothetical]

For the sake of this
mathematical hypothetical,
I'm a federal bus marshal
here to monitor
the inconsiderate-guy-
in-the-bathroom situation.
Represent variables
in the following manner:
let b stand for the bladder control
of the goat crated
above the lounger.
The number of hours
I've camped outside the bathroom
like an antsy golfer awaiting the green
should be rounded
to the nearest hundred.
Some call me Slobath the Destroyer
after my exploits
aboard Megabus 559,
but for the sake of this word problem,
consider me and my deputy,
played by the ghost of Boris Karloff,

the last commandos of civility.
He should be shattering plates
in the kitchen
of an elderly debutante
or testing tacks
on deserted highways,
but instead he signals me
to move into position.
We initiate
Freedom Protocol (f)
which involves
kicking and screaming
and is all that separates us
from lampreys
suckling cans of beans,
I shout, as we maul the suspect.
Represent the subject as a stoic teen
who's been nursing a nectarine
since Iowa City.
If t equals the tightness
of my handcuffs,
how long will it be
until our mutual appetite
for destruction abates?
Until we're across state lines
exploding stygian archipelagos
along the highway
where your life
as a tender hellcat is over?

III. You Were Born to Graze

[When a man loves a woman, he will be asked: Soup or salad]

When a man loves a woman,
he will be asked: Soup or salad?
And though he has trained
his whole life for this,
the man will inquire
about the soup of the day
like the black angel of dichotomies.
Days can't survive here,
the waiter replies.
We're slumming it around the rough-
and-tumble hood of a black hole.
Or more precisely, adds another waiter
polishing some silver,
we're trapped inside
an artist's rendition of a black hole.
Thus the stilted elephants
crushing bystanders.
Thus the Dada hitching posts protruding
from your rapidly expanding wings.
And by this point,
the soup is cold
and sliding toward the void.

Massive abysses coalesce above the fans
absorbing bouquets of hyacinths.
Maybe, suggests the artist,
who up to this point
has remained silent,
the soup nebula
is colliding with the salad belt
bounding its brothy ellipses.
This collision is forming varied
whole-wheat and kale anomalies.
Maybe, suggests the man,
we are all just victims of one another
in one fashion or another.
Then the cops bust in
and begin blackjacking everyone.
Shattered plates litter the floor.
How hard it has been
to love like this.

[It happens like this]

It happens like this:
Today, the monks
on the slopes of my aorta
swear their vows of narcolepsy,
promise one asleep
on the job incident.
Then I see a sign
with the word banana
beside a picture of a banana
and cross myself
for Michel Foucault
who is still out there, people,
breathlessly hunting
the squirmy-wormy beast
of teeny-bopper surfer flicks.
I'm fighting, really, to maintain control
over this wheelbarrow of feeling
these mountains are way too far up.
What's it to you
if I christen this Forklift
Operated Under Divine
Influence Mountain?
Or Mt. Doe with Eyes Shot Out?
You're just two chemically

bonded protons
in a seventh grade science book
holding the hand of a pretty girl
who looks unhappy.

[Omaha, what besides animals on loan can you offer]

Omaha, what besides animals
on loan can you offer?
Eric's Extreme Body Shaping,
mobile meth kitchens.
Your suitors
prefer the fakest names:
Taniel, Tessica.
They don oversized yellow hats
like this open pasture
isn't a place of business.
But they have another thing coming, Omaha.
Yesterday, I misherded your cows
and now the whole field
might as well be the moon.
They cultivate the kind of boredom
only prey could love.
When I visit you,
I expect a little more than tapirs,
antelope, parrots
and over fifty varieties of wild cat.
I put on your worn folk ballads.
You put on your beautiful emptiness,

and no one notices.
How alike we've grown.
I feel like the lone
publically-funded snake pit
in America.
Those evenings
when I slither so sweet,
that tight coil you feel
around your thorax
is more than
mere instinct to touch.
It's joy.

[Forsake your foolish quest, you pleaded]

Forsake your foolish quest,
you pleaded, and retire
to the rough-and-tumble
streets where you were born.
It had been a hard September,
cavorting across the horizon
with its pink and sinking contentment
bedding down in dirty laundromats
and waking to the machine hum
of a headache.
After five months,
what did I have to show?
Some Farrah Fawcett swimwear,
a fifty dollar gift card.
My name is Mighty Beast McCord
I cried, and all I've ever done
was out of love.
You nodded, stroking my arm,
loosing the makeshift knout
from my grip.
You knew this invocation well.
All I wanted
was for you to like me,
at the exact moment

that I discover
the Spanish word for panda
is panda and stare off a sea cliff
where a head of cattle nibbles
on the sun's prayer shawl,
not in a hungry way
but as if they were huffing
the most magisterial cud.

[When you've been scoutmaster as a long as I have]

When you've been scoutmaster
as long as I have,
every fire is a child
with blueberry stains on its lips.
Every mispitched tent,
a safety exposé of the sleaziest order
just waiting to be filmed.
When the ghost of Thurgood Marshall
comes waltzing into your office
like some liquored-up jackhammer,
you've got bigger places to be—
at the top of a pine,
or perfecting marching orders
for the third plastic infantry.
The rumors about the tiny Christmas lights
lodged in my soul are true.
Even on foggy nights,
this illumination threatens to combust
all I hold dear.
When I turned to the American Cougar
Appreciation Society for help,
I anticipated more fang-gnashing

carcass-dragging action.
But you seem nice.
When you've been scoutmaster
as long as I have,
you can tell a good one.
These merit badges
practically pin themselves.
On long nights, the campsite
appears one big ghost town,
with you forever cast
as the last halfway
decent mountaineer.

[Inside a dog it is too dark to read]

Inside a dog it is too dark to read,
but who could prove it?
A vole, the shredded remnants
of a paper towel roll.
I can hear big ole life
happening outside me,
but I can't see it.
Schrödinger's cat intrudes
into metaphysics.
The not-knowing keeps me
creasing the pages
one by one as I go.
I say, put on
your gardening gloves
and cleansing crème,
it's time.
The heat of Texas with its ear
to the ground listens for a train.
Rain in the gutters, no longer rain,
glitters into the abyss.
What is uncertain remains
beside the smoothest crest
of skyline smirked by a river

without a single thing to lose
itself inside.

[I may never understand why you purchased the bonnet]

I may never understand
why you purchased the bonnet
embroidered with a nude merman,
but you'll always have my respect.
This convention has changed
the way I think about my employment
in Evil Law Firm #5.
Such a gaggle of winos they attract!
Watch as they wobble into view
like some poor spirograph.
Maybe there is a great hand
pointing at each person's heart.
I can't be totally sure.
In the banquet halls of Krakow,
one greets each day
with such certainty.
Prosecutors curse
each suit coat's insulation.
But don't fault the solar giant
for doing its job
advertising sun tan lotion
for Evil Corporate Client #2.

So what if it returns each day
disguised as a beggar
here to thwart lusty suitors?
That's what it's paid to do.

[In the event of an emergency, the gallons of Gatorade]

In the event of an emergency,
the gallons of Gatorade
in the overhead compartment
will automatically detonate,
so we can all go down like champs.
So, here's to the thirst quencher.
Here's to the finest elevator tune
ever to go airborne.
Here in your seat back pocket,
you'll find a sample will
illustrating possible delegations
of earthly possessions:
To the salt in the wound,
I bequeath my disappointments.
To my eighth grade jazz ensemble,
my undying wrath
which hovers
like a malicious hummingbird
haranguing an atrium.
To those limping,
those engaged in the inventory
of sturgeon nests

for purposes of census collection,
I leave my stock options
and commemorative hill giant.
You'll find my native woods
unkempt and askew.
You'll find your days there pleasant
in spite of the petulant cawing.
To those caterwauling,
those taking the chump train
to Suckersville,
your stop will be on the right
as you exit the aircraft.
Your squawking has roused
those nascent babies,
human French horns.
Their mounting chorus threatens
what little sanity
we've managed to preserve
by sealing it in time-safe jars
for future generations
of tomb raiders
to admire and enjoy.

[The Denny's was divided into spheres of influence]

The Denny's was divided
into spheres of influence,
but peace increasingly reminded me
of an atoll awaiting nuclear testing.
In the first sphere,
Satan was an orphan
peering in the bakery window.
In the second, tweens modeled
the unsexiest kind of love.
I ruled the smoking sector
because I was behind the wheel
of the minivan
that collapsed the entryway.
In the past, I'd been acclaimed
for my freelance warlording.
But now, covered in rubble,
my twitchy citizens
had grown only twitchier.
Treaty lines blocked
our access to pastries.
I was under arrest by authorities.
There's still time to be young

and awake in a different music video
than you fell asleep in, I shouted.
But they take massive, reckless
property damage seriously
here in Pennsylvania.
Not even Satan's sniveling
can change that.
I raised my hand
in query, in dissent
but the officers
were in a holiday mood.
Maybe you out there
have many questions also.
Perhaps you think starlight's
some form of pity.

[Maybe it's bullet day or eat-a-lamb day]

Maybe it's bullet day
or eat-a-lamb day
and no one has remembered
to unchain me
from the troubadour's corpse.
This could explain
the sheer quantity of gunfire
but not the lack of shady,
Ruisdael-ian forests
for a fellow to wander.
Maybe today you and I
will take on the task
of simultaneously fearing
everything at once.
A picnic basket with iced scones
and turtle soup
will terrorize us
to the point of absolute fullness.
And if mutants opt to dance around us
with their horrifying mutant hands,
well isn't that their right?
Some mutant may shout,
No one will ever hurt me again!
And here, amidst the shell casings

and lamb carcasses,
we'll know it can't last.
But I'll take out my dusty lamp
and light it for you still,
true believer.

Acknowledgments

American Letters and Commentary: [I had no intention to retire from soothsaying] and [Once they evacuate the impromptu rodeo]

Barn Owl Review: [You can redeem yourself by helping me slay]

Barrow Street: [It happens like this]

Burnside Review: [It was in those days]

The Collagist: [I may never understand why you purchased the bonnet]

Denver Quarterly: [Last night I heard the frail music of nighthawks], [Even when I solicited Satan with affordable snow tires, he listened], and [This is no time for grandiose displays of pinball prowess]

Forklift, Ohio: [I swear this is the last time I'm going into space]

Fou: [Last night I heard the yowls of the listless jaguar]

Hayden's Ferry Review: [For the sake of this mathematical hypothetical]

Jellyfish: [When you've scoutmaster as long as I have]

The Journal: [When a man loves a woman, he sits her down]

The Laurel Review: [I'd like to take a minute to honor the ordinary]

Linebreak: [When a man loves a woman, he will be asked: Soup or salad]

Memorious: [Omaha, what besides animals on loan can you offer]

New Orleans Review: [Perhaps this day marks the end of your kayak internship]

OH NO: [When a man loves a woman, they journey]

Passages North: [In the event of an emergency, the gallons of Gatorade]

Pebble Lake Review: [If you won't swear to remarry me in the afterlife]

Poetry Northwest: [Put down that pint of human blood and tell me you need me] and [The Denny's was divided into spheres of influence]

Sixth Finch: [Inside a dog it is too dark to read]

Slice: [Maybe it's bullet day or eat-a-lamb day] and [Forsake your foolish quest, you pleaded]

TriQuarterly: [In this scene, my co-pilot and I crash the moonbuggy]

Verse: [If you're reading this, I forgive you for eating me first]

Verse Daily: [For the sake of this mathematical hypothetical]

Whiskey Island: [On my bucket list: don't do anything miraculous] and [The snow whirs like another planet's machinery]

Kyle McCord is the author of three books of poetry: *Galley of the Beloved in Torment* (Dream Horse Press 2009) winner of 2008 Orphic Prize, a co-written book of epistolary poems entitled *Informal Invitations to a Traveler* (Gold Wake Press 2011) and *Sympathy from the Devil* (Gold Wake Press, 2013). He has work featured in *Boston Review*, *Denver Quarterly*, *Gulf Coast*, *Third Coast*, *TriQuarterly* and elsewhere. He's received grants or awards from the Academy of American Poets, the Vermont Studio Center, and the Iowa Poetry Association. He's the 2012 recipient of the Baltic Writing Residence. He is the co-founder of *American Microreviews and Interviews,* and he co-edits *iO: A Journal of New American Poetry*. He lives and teaches in Des Moines, Iowa.

About the Cover Artist:

Robyn O'Neil was born in Omaha, Nebraska in 1977, and currently lives in Los Angeles, California. Her work was included in the 2004 Whitney Biennial. She is the recipient of numerous grants and awards, including a Joan Mitchell Foundation Grant. O'Neil has had several traveling solo museum exhibitions in the United States, and has been included in numerous acclaimed group museum exhibitions both domestically and internationally. She also received a grant from the Irish Film Board for a film written and art directed by her entitled "WE, THE MASSES" which was conceived of at Werner Herzog's Rogue Film School.

CPSIA information can be obtained
at www.ICGtesting.com
Printed in the USA
FFOW02n2316300415
13087FF